Vessels of Strength

Can you hear me now?

Screaming into destiny!

Amber N. Hearn, DMFT

Ernest Griffin, B.A.

Phorode Brown, B.S.

Emanuel Officer, Ph.D.

The Stanton Book Company
Palm Springs, California
stantonbooks.net
Printed in the United States of America

"Be strong and courageous; do not be afraid; do not be discouraged, for the Lord your God will be with you wherever you go."

Joshua 1:9

Contents

Preface   i

Introduction: Introduction:
The Purpose of This Book   iii

Chapter 1: From "Ernie" to "Ernest":   1
The Development of a Successful
African American Male

Chapter 2: A Few Systems To Put In Place   27

Chapter 3: There Are No Coincidences or Ironies   37

Chapter 4: Steps to Succeed in College   47

Chapter 5: Experiencing Racism in College   51

Chapter 6: Key Concepts to Remember   59

Chapter 7: Vessels of Strength, Prayer,   75
And The Covering

Chapter 8: Are You A Vessel of Strength?   87
How to Become A *Vessels of Strength*
Member

Vessels of Strength Membership Application   89
Author Biographies   91
Acknowledgments
Bibliography

Preface

This book, *Vessels of Strength*, encapsulates the emotional, intellectual, mental and spiritual strength of three, African American men who illustrate their personal journeys to success.

When Dr. Amber N. Hearn was a doctoral student, she read literature concerning the struggles and hardships African American men face as they attempt to navigate through higher education.

Due to these revelations, she was exhausted and appalled after reading about the struggle of her African American brothers, without the accompaniment of success. Dr. Amber N. Hearn agrees that obstacles are inevitable, but she also believes accepting them, learning and being motivated by them, leads to victory.

The introduction and body of *Vessels of Strength* provides you with an overview of the importance of shining a light on the victories of African American men, while also understanding how they persevered, despite their adversities.

The body of this book reveals the personal journey of each author. We encourage and support our readers to acknowledge, accept, and use their challenges toward success in meeting their goals. *Vessels of Strength* ends with a prayer and encouraging words entitled, "The Covering." This prayer will build faith in each reader to find, perform and enjoy their purpose in life.

We've also included an invitation for you to join *Vessels of Strength* and allow your light to shine, by sharing your story and/or becoming a mentor.

Introduction:

The Purpose of this Book

By Dr. Amber N. Hearn

As the founder of *Vessels of Strength*, God has truly given me a heart to provide a space for African American male voices to be heard relative to their successes. I was inspired to publish a book based on both, the *Vessels of Strength* Facebook social media page I created in 2014, and the literature review I completed for my research course in my doctoral program, as a student at Loma Linda University.

The purpose of this social media page is to support my African American brothers in Christ by providing a safe place for their voices to be heard concerning their personal and educational success. This page is also designed to create an online community for African American males (AAM) to engage with other, like-minded individuals within their own ethnic background. Research and social media frequently raise the issues of African American men dropping out of college.

I also learned limited credit is given to those who successfully complete and obtain their Bachelor's Degrees and beyond. What I mean by this is: Black men with some college and/or Bachelor's Degrees are not often statistically recognized.

Like our social media site, this book, *Vessels of Strength,* provides African American men an opportunity to have their opinions, stories and journeys acknowledged without being criticized and belittled. In addition, the purpose of this book is to be uplifting and encouraging to these men, to discuss their accomplishments and goals. It adds to the mentorship journey, not only for our young men under 18-years-old, but to extend support and mentorship to AAM who entered adulthood and later life stages.

While my efforts are to support my African American brothers in revealing their inner strength, my spiritual inspiration is derived from the first book of the Gospel in the Bible, Matthew 5:16. "Let your light so shine before men, that they may see your good works, and glorify your Father which is in heaven."

In this book, three African American males, who are also *Vessels of Strength* members, discuss their past, present, and future successes; despite their many challenges. They also shared how the Lord carried them through this journey, while educating readers on how they too can pursue and accomplish their academic and personal dreams. Like this book, the literature review I completed for my doctoral research course, motivated me to not only write this, but also submit an article in a peer review journal. I am currently in the process of editing this article, which I hope will depict my passion for promoting the successes and struggles AAM face, along their personal journeys to reveal their own experiences and definitions of success.

This article currently discusses the nationwide crisis of low retention rates of AAM in undergraduate programs. It's highlighted in this document that Harper (2012) and Suggs (2012) report 57% of AAM drop out of college, due to a variety of risk factors impacting their achievement of graduating.

The article offers a more in-depth understanding of the internal and external challenges AAM experience while progressing through their undergraduate level programs. Further, a narrative, conceptual framework is used to discuss how AAM can overcome these challenges. The steps included focus on creating:

(1) support groups;

(2) self-development classes and workshops; and

(3) mentorship programs.

This critical literature review acknowledges and also focuses on the need to incorporate therapeutic programs on college campuses, which would help to increase retention rates for AAM in college, teach work/life management, support individuals in adapting to independence, and so much more.

Lastly, this review discusses core steps that social change agents can take to implement healing treatment strategies in higher educational systems for AAM.

Like the outline of this upcoming article, I strongly pray this book not only reveals the personal and academic lives of each author, but that each reader is shifted in their thinking: to believe, inspire hope, encouragement, motivation, and offer platform strategies to support my African American brothers to succeed in their academic and personal lives. The intent of *Vessels of Strength* is for readers to feel encouraged to tell their story to the world, while also pursuing their lifelong dreams.

I encourage all readers to reach out to *Vessels of Strength* if you are looking for a mentor, or would like to become a mentor, and engage with our social media community, as follows:

Email:

vesselsofstrength@gmail.com

Social media community:

Vessels of Strength Facebook page:

https://www.facebook.com/AfricanAmerican
MenVesselsofStrength/

Chapter 1

From "Ernie" to "Ernest"

The Development of
A Successful African American Male

By Ernest Griffin

My struggles as an African American male (AAM) growing up in the inner city were tough. Luckily, with God, well-rounded parents, and the support of my family, I was able to get through the many challenges my life presented.

At the early age of five, I was diagnosed with attention-deficit-hyperactivity disorder (ADHD) and I didn't know what that meant at the time, but as I got older, I eventually became aware of what ADHD involved. As I continued to move up into different grade levels, I noticed things got more challenging for me, like reading, spelling, comprehending things and my ability to think quickly. I first noticed the issue when I was in the third grade. Back then, it seemed like all the kids in my class were smarter than me and I was always a step or two behind them. I remember when it came down to taking different tests, I never seemed to do well, no matter how much I studied or prepared for the tests. To me, it always seemed like I came up short of getting a passing grade.

When it came to reading books at my grade level, I could never seem to comprehend what I was reading because I had poor reading skills to begin with; hence, I hated reading books. However, I did notice that I was good at math! I was also good at copying from other students' papers when it came to taking test.

One day, I walked into class on a Friday, which was test day. We had an entire week to study and prepare. I remember walking over to my desk, nervously, not knowing what was on this test. All I knew was, whoever sat beside me would be the first person I was going to cheat off.

In the back of my mind, I had everything already mapped and planned out for what I was going to do, even before we started taking the test. The only thing that made me nervous was getting caught and having to go to the principal's office. As soon as we started the test, I began to lose my mind. I knew only a few of the answers to the questions. After a few minutes, I quickly glanced left at my classmate's paper for answers; then glanced again to the right, to see what they'd written on their papers.

Then, I turned forward to look at my own paper and-- *Bam!* My third grade teacher caught me cheating red handed! She sent me to the principal's office for copying off my classmate's test. This didn't seem like a big deal to me because I'd been cheating on tests for quite some time. I had already gotten caught cheating a couple times before. This time, however, the stakes were higher, and this visit was no ordinary one to the principal's office. This time, I was sent home and suspended for a couple days.

When I arrived back at school, I was put into a new class and assigned a new teacher. Things in this new class were different because the special teacher introduced me to many different materials I wasn't used to.

As time passed, I noticed that I wasn't interacting with the same friends anymore and I realized I'd been placed in a 'special class.' Here, I blended in well with many of the students who, like myself, could barely read and comprehend things as fast as the other students. As time progressed, I steadily adapted to my new learning disability.

As I got older and continued to move forward with ADHD, I learned how to accept it. I always told myself I would never let anyone get the best of me due to this disability. I always did whatever I could to hide this from everyone. Once the other children became aware of this, they used it against me to hurt my feelings. Once I graduated from elementary, I moved on to junior high, which bought me into a whole new world.

In elementary school, everyone was just being kids and enjoying their youth. My childhood consisted of playing handball, kickball, hide and seek, and--tag, you're it. All these are fun childhood memories that everyone can relate to because being a kid was just about playing and having fun. Junior high was a totally different ball game.

To me, this transition into junior high was like a movie rating. My elementary years were all parentally guided, but in middle school things changed to 'Rated R.' Being in junior high was a game-changer for me, because the school was bigger (along with the shapes and sizes of the students).

There was more than just one class and there were way more students than I'd ever seen before. The campus also had a lot of security. I thought this was kind of odd since I never saw security guards at the elementary school. It took some time for me to get adjusted to junior high school because there was so much to absorb. I had to get familiar with my classes, teachers, the layout of the campus, my classmates, and the homework I received on various subjects almost every day. This was a big challenge for me because I was also involved with other activities, like playing basketball and running track. I even attended music class and played the saxophone.

I was good at playing music. That was the only thing I got right during school. Learning and playing the saxophone was the one thing *I loved* outside of playing sports. I also loved talking to my classmates, playing video games during class, and reading comic books instead of my regular schoolbooks. Because of these slackened choices, my performance in class and my grades began to decline.

One day, while taking an English test, my teacher noticed I had gotten low scores on my tests and that I always got my words mixed up when trying to write a complete sentence. So, my English teacher decided to place me into a different class where I'd receive the specialized help I needed. Over time my reading, writing, and comprehension skills began to improve. While taking this special class, I learned a few things about myself as well. I learned that I was still behind, I still couldn't read at my grade level, and that I still had a lot to overcome in a short period of time.

Over the years, I realized growing up as a Black man with a learning disability in today's world, I'd have to work twice as hard as the next person, just to make it in this life. The things I went through in elementary, junior high and high school were the foundation I needed to overcome the daily challenges life brought. The stereotypes that portray African American men in social media and society are, and have been, negative for the most part.

During my high school years, I learned that no matter what people may say about you, you must learn to avoid their criticism and *continue moving forward!* Not every Black male is a thug, gangster, pimp, thief, drug-dealer, or con-man. Yet, I believe I am labeled with these characteristics on a regular basis.

While there are many characteristics that society depicts concerning Black men, I don't see myself the way certain elements of society see me. I am a civilized, educated individual who wants nothing but the best for myself and generations to come. *I am one of those individuals!*

It took a while for me to figure out that I must better myself in order to help others. The most challenging as well as fulfilling times of my life were my high school and subsequent college years. During these years, I discovered myself and who I wanted to be.

I faced common AAM challenges and my own personal ones. Today, I'm a college graduate with a Bachelor of Arts Degree in Communications, and still work toward reaching my highest academic and professional potential. My road was by far not an easy one, but I have no regrets. My obstacles, good and bad, made me who I am today.

Who am I? I am a successful AAM who conquered a learning disability and obtained a college degree, while managing to resist peer pressures and avoid a life of crime. I owe my success to God, my parents and my family who never gave up on me. My story is no different from many others, but if it will help just one struggling student, it is worth telling. Here is the condensed version of my personal journey from "Ernie" to "Ernest."

After junior high, I knew I'd have to grow up and start being a little more responsible for myself and my actions; meaning, I had stop blaming others for my own failures and start being more responsible and independent. For me, this meant doing my homework without being told, helping out Mom around the house by doing my chores, being more focused in class, and making sure I asked for help whenever I needed it, in order to do well in all my classes.

Thank God I had great parents who were strict but reasonable! Having a father around showed me what it was like to be *a man*, and how to face challenges head on, no matter what the circumstances. My father helped me realize that nothing came easy in life, and that I must work hard to achieve whatever it is I wanted out of life. My dad worked many jobs to get what he wanted out of life. He was a teacher, a coach at his school, and he also cut lawns to earn extra money.

Although he didn't spend much time with me growing up, I realized he was too busy out there working, trying to provide for himself and his family. I learned how a true man should stand in life from my Dad. He taught me five things:

1. Be responsible for your own actions
2. Be honest
3. Be helpful
4. Be a provider
5. Be a leader

Learning these life lessons from my dad, I realized I must continue to carry out all these things and apply them to my daily life in order to be successful. When I encountered different challenges in my life, like dealing with bullies and community gang members, my older cousin, Jay, was also one of those fatherly men who led me the right way. Jay helped raise me as a young man. He was always there with good, helpful advice, like, how to deal with bullies at school and how to avoid joining a gang.

He told me that being in a gang is not the way. "It's nothing but problems and consequences that come with the position, and it's not worth losing your life over." He continued, "Being in a gang does not make you the big man on the block, or popular. It just brings drama and headaches."

I remember in my freshman year of high school, there was this one bully, a sophomore, who played football on the junior varsity team. This bully used to live on my aunt's block, but he moved away once I entered junior high. This guy was pretty tall and I was shorter than him. When he stood right next to me, it was like standing next to Shaq (from the Lakers).

I really couldn't understand why he loved messing with me every time he saw me. He always tried to steal my snacks during lunch, punk me for my lunch money, and then make fun of me for being short and chubby. And then one day, I got sick and tired of this guy picking on me, so I went to the one person I knew could help me out; my cousin Jay.

Jay always had helpful advice for me. He told me not to back down, no matter how intimidating this guy was. "Stand your ground and show no fear!" Jay taught me that I had to show this bully I was no coward because the strong always prey on the weak in order to feel superior.

You must be willing to stand tall, look that bully in the eye and say, "Enough is enough!" Let them know who you are and be ready for whatever happens next. With the help from my cousin, I was able to confront my bully like a man. I told him, "I will not let you take control of me and I will no longer put up with your disrespect." At that moment, we rushed toward one another and started going at it.

At the end, I got my butt kicked but that was the last day that bully messed around with me. He now knew that I wasn't a little punk anymore, and I wasn't afraid to face him again, no matter what. Without my cousin Jay's knowledge and wisdom, I probably wouldn't have gotten through that bully situation at school.

My first day of school at Junipero Serra High was spent looking at all the new faces, all the nationalities, weird and crazy styles, and students of various shapes and sizes walking around campus. The atmosphere was cool, but I still felt a little funny because I didn't have any of my old friends with me. It was me, alone, for the first time. The only recognizable difference was the girls; they were way better looking!

Not to mention, the food selection was a lot better in the cafeteria! High school was additionally challenging because of puberty. Everything I learned prior about staying focused and asking for help when I needed it, were now thrown out the window. I had the hardest time staying focused. Anything and everything easily distracted me, and it reflected upon my grades. I also lacked motivation. I just wanted to be cool.

I constantly checked my cell phone, cracked jokes to get the class laughing, and other little, annoying things because I didn't understand the class topic, or I was just plain bored. Hanging around class clowns didn't help either, because we always sat in the back of the class cracking jokes on anything and anyone who seemed to be dressed differently, or looked out of place. For instance, we clowned on students for wearing fake Jordan's, Gucci, and Nautica gear.

Peer pressure was another distraction for me in high school. I felt being cool and accepted would make me feel better about myself. I soon noticed that certain friends who were not focused on their studies and not involved in any extracurricular activities, were the problem. They didn't use their time engaged in things like homework and going to practice. Instead, they smoked, drank and committed crimes to keep themselves busy. Luckily, I figured out that was not the crowd for me. I knew deep down inside that I wanted more for myself. I knew I must stay focused on school and continue consistently in my sports activities, like football and track. With all I had going on in my life, and with good people surrounding me, I knew I would continue my journey and finish high school.

Academic life at Junipero Serra was also different in that I didn't have the support team I had in previous years. In the public-school system, my ADHD allowed me to have a good support team and different resources to make learning easier. Since Junipero Serra was a private high school, I had to forfeit those luxuries. I had to use my common sense and try much harder to focus and study on my own. I admit it was hard. There were times I had difficulties grasping certain concepts about schoolwork and teacher assignments.

Luckily, my Mom was always there for me when I needed her the most. She helped me with the majority of my schoolwork and class projects by giving me the proper tools necessary, like pens, pencils, glue, poster boards, 3-ring binders and much more; the typical school supply list. With my Mom as a big support system, I knew I couldn't fail because she was always there to help me out.

Other times, I got help from my cousins, Regina and Denethia. In fact, they were working on teaching degrees and knew different teaching approaches. They knew what I needed to do to get through my classes and shared that knowledge with me.

I learned to manage my time and not overexert myself. I also learned to ask for help as soon as I got confused instead of waiting until I failed a test. Most importantly, I learned that all I can do is my best, and everything else will fall in line. I listened, and those techniques helped me to get through, which proved to be a turning point in my life. I realized that I too can be successful—and that I would be.

In private school there weren't many students. The campus space was smaller, not many teachers to choose from, not as many activities going on as in public school, and you had to pay your way.

My first year was a little challenging because I had to make new friends all over again. A lot of the friends I graduated with from junior high moved on through public school programs. So, now I was on my own, taking on this new journey by myself in my first year of high school. I noticed that I needed to get myself more involved with different activities in order to make new friends and get used to the private school system which I wasn't used to at all. I joined a music class and got involved in an after-school sports club where everyone who loved sports stayed involved with all the sports activities going on at campus.

My first and second year of high school, I remember that I went through so many different phases, I didn't even recognize who I was anymore. I went through a phase of carelessness, where I didn't care about other people's feelings or how I treated them, because I was trying to be cool or popular in front of those I thought were cool.

I was disrespectful, heartless and gave the teachers a rough time by clowning around all the time; much like I had in the past. I started hanging with the wrong crowd and doing things I had absolutely no business doing, while trying to fit in. Almost every time I hung around those friends, I found myself in trouble or in the Dean's office.

I don't know why the others acted out, but I was disrespectful to teachers because I didn't understand. I purposely interrupted the class and ended up at the Dean's office numerous times. Sometimes, when the teacher sent us to the Dean, he just looked at us and shook his head in disappointment, as if we were just a waste of space. Other times, he called home and told my Mom I was acting a fool in class and being disrespectful. Then, I knew I was in trouble.

I will never forget the never-ending ride home. It was on a Thursday afternoon. My mom and I were on our way home from school. Mom had this straight look on her face, as if she was going to hit me right there. I'd been acting a fool in school again and close to getting kicked out. My Mom was really upset with me. It almost seemed as though she was about to cry. Junipero Serra was one of the best schools in the area for which she spent all her hard-earned money to place me in.

That day I realized I must change my act and get it together because if I continued getting in trouble, I would end up at some public school where the teachers were crappy, and the students were even more rude and disrespectful than me. So, I promised my mother I would get my act together, stop acting like a class clown and start doing better for myself. I also promised I'd get all the help I needed in order to get through high school.

That night I prayed. I asked the Lord's forgiveness and to help guide me through life as a teenager, because I was really starting to lose myself. Junipero Serra High School was like being a part of a small family, which made it easier for me to get to know people, even though I was still a little shy. The first thing I did was, make sure to leave my class clown buddies alone and start paying more attention to what the teacher had to say in class. I stayed on a little extra time after class if I didn't get something during the lecture, or if I misunderstood the subject. I also started to study more and spent less time on video games. I also got a tutor for extra help in the subjects I was doing poorly in. Going through all these new changes, helped me get through my freshman year at Serra, and the rest of the years ahead. I've learned not to be a follower because 'following' got me nowhere but in trouble, and almost kicked out of school.

During my second year, I learned to have faith in my abilities to do whatever I wanted; which was to get good grades in school and stay out of trouble. My third year, I learned that I had to put in the work in order to accomplish my goals.

In my senior year of high school, I learned that hard work, dedication, and discipline helped me get far in life and to where I wanted to be. As I went through my teenage transitions, I always looked up to my parents, my older brother, Sherman, and my older cousin, Jay, for advice.

My parents were awesome role models because they never did anything negative in front of me like smoke, drink, or disrespect each other. They also showed me that with hard work and determination, anything I wanted to do is possible in life. I just had to believe in myself and get it done.

With help from my family, I stayed out of trouble, away from the wrong crowd and off the streets.

I thank the Lord for putting people like them in my life. They were family members who'd been through many of the same challenges and situations I was going through at the time.

With knowledge and proper guidance, I was able to overcome many pitfalls in life. That is why I stayed prayed up and away from all negativity. I knew that had I gotten around the wrong people and involved in the wrong things, I probably would never have graduated from high school.

While still attending high school, my mother got me involved in many different activities: sports, music; anything to keep me out of trouble. One of the programs that really helped me develop as a person was the Customs Cadet Program; an outstanding program for teens interested in law enforcement.

This program taught individuals desiring to grow and develop their skills in leadership, confidence, self-motivation and discipline, while learning the importance of teamwork. I picked up a lot of different skills and learned a lot about myself and my capabilities in the Customs Cadet Program. It taught me how to be organized, efficient and punctual. If we came late to training, or were out of uniform, we had to do 50 to 100 push-ups, or write a 3 to 5-page paper explaining why we were late and out of uniform.

This type of discipline helped me be on time to my classes, music and football practice. It also taught me to be well-groomed, take pride in my appearance and value my self-worth. I also learned how to believe in myself and be a leader.

Graduating from Junipero Serra High School was the entrance of a new path to my future which, in this case, was attending El Camino Junior College. Now, I would be on my own to make different decisions. The decisions I had to make began with deciding when to go to class, when to do my homework, eat whatever I wanted, and hangout with whomever I wanted; instead of someone dictating how I was supposed to act. It was now all on me to determine how my future would turn out, without supervision or anyone telling me what to do and when to do it. Everything I wanted to accomplish out of life was now up to me.

I learned that focus and determination will take you far in life, if you stay on the right path. Going from high school to college is like graduating from an immature youngster to a mature adult, because you now have more responsibilities and challenges ahead.

Moving into higher learning for me meant more difficult work and longer nights of studying; still not knowing what I really wanted to do with my life, but I continued to push myself, regardless.

College wasn't really a big deal to me at first. My Mom told me I was the first male from my generation on her side of the family to go to college. So, I made it my purpose to complete my degree. Although my family didn't have much money to support me in school, I did my best to work hard and make good grades so I could get a student grant and help pay for my higher education.

I knew the Lord was the one I could call on for help at any time. I always prayed to the Lord for help. I asked him for strength and blessings, while I tried to move forward with school. I asked God to grant me the strength to resist any possible distractions from reaching my goals.

My first year of college was a big eye-opener. This is where I met different people from all nationalities, religions, and cultures who focused on one thing: their education. It was totally different. No one told you what to do and how to do it. There were no separate groups, no one picking on you for being different and no drama. College was definitely a different atmosphere. I was in a world where no one cared about social status and everyone was there to help one another achieve their goals. During my freshman year at El Camino Junior College, I enrolled in a program called, Project Success. This program was designed for minorities who needed a little guidance and a push to help them get through college. It was a very good program that helped students like myself get the classes I needed and tutors, along with special discounts on books and supplies to help me out at school. The program assigned each student to a counselor and mentor to help guide us through the semester. The staff in the program were helpful and knowledgeable toward students and got them the support they needed. The staff also made sure we enrolled on time every semester and that we got the classes we needed in order to finish school within 2 to 3 years.

My counselor, Professor Smith, taught Psychology 101. He was an outstanding mentor. It seemed like, whatever I was going through in school, he always had an answer or solution to help me solve my problems. I remember, once I enrolled into the wrong class, and the Political History class I needed was already full. It was a class that I needed to take in order to graduate on time! So, I went to my counselor to get some advice, and he told me to go to the class and ask the teacher politely if I could sit in on a couple of classes to see if anyone would eventually drop out so that I could fill that space. Surely, after a week, some of the students dropped the class and I was able to enroll. Thanks to my mentor, Professor Smith's helpful advice, I was able to get the credits I needed to ensure my timely graduation! While in the Project Success Program, in addition to my counselor, I was assigned to a mentor, named Dr. Spearman; an African American English and History professor who held Masters' and Doctorate Degrees. Dr. Spearman was about six feet tall with a short fade and a bald spot on the top of his head. His body was a regular build (as if he went to the gym only twice a week), and he wore glasses that made him look like JJ from "Good Times," but with a smaller head.

Dr. Spearman was a great mentor, teacher and friend who also cared about the education of others. He wasn't just some ordinary English teacher. This guy was a highly intelligent, knowledgeable person who knew a lot about life. He helped me get through a lot of my classes at El Camino College by making sure I stayed on top of my homework assignments, and he met with me every two weeks to see how I was doing. Dr. Spearman gave me helpful advice like, making sure I went over all my classwork twice to ensure I had done everything correctly.

He also bought me a daily planner and sat down with me to make sure I knew and understood exactly how to plan out my day according to my classes and job schedule.

I was working full-time at Macy's at the time. As a teacher, he taught me that procrastination will always throw me behind, and it will take longer to catch up with the rest. So, every time I turned in a late assignment in his class he'd say, "If you want to be a success in life you must learn how to turn your work in on time, and stop waiting until the last minute to finish up everything because it will determine your grade and the outcome of passing or failing this class."

He spoke very matter-of-factly to me, and yet, Dr. Spearman was like a friend throughout the program. He was always available and helpful when it came to good advice. When things got tough for me to handle some of my classes, while working full-time, he was the one who told me that I needed to quit my full-time job and find a part-time job; either on campus or somewhere near the campus. This way, he explained, I would be able to manage my time better.

I also remember when I wasn't doing so well in the Political History class, he advised me to get extra help and go talk to the teacher to see what I could do to bring my grades back up; like extra homework, or even working on an extra class project by myself to help boost my grades. No matter what issue I had at school or in my classes, Dr. Spearman was always there to encourage me, to push through it and find different ways to improve myself and my education.

There was a time when I wanted to drop Spanish class. It was hard for me to pick-up the language. I had to do a lot of extra reading and writing to master the language enough to pass the class. So, I told Dr. Spearman that I wanted to drop out of the class, but he encouraged me to hang in there and find a classmate or buddy who spoke Spanish, to help me with this subject.

When I told him that I tried that and I still wasn't doing well, he found one of the counselors within the Project Success Programs who spoke Spanish to help me get through all the work and class projects. With a little bit of extra help, I was able to pass the class and move forward to the next semester.

Due to all the wisdom and advice I received from Dr. Spearman, I realized it's OK to ask for help. Because of Dr. Spearman's support, I value family, friends, teachers, and mentors' advice today, and continued support throughout my life-long journey. Every time I was close to dropping out, Dr. Spearman told me…

> "There's no decent future for a brotha' without a degree!"

And:

"Procrastination will always hurt you if you're not prepared for what's ahead of you in the long run."

In other words, if you wait to the last minute to do something, you'll always be behind. Having a mentor like Dr. Spearman while attending college helped me to appreciate all those I had around me, and the resources available to help me get through school.

Dr. Spearman helped me realize that you need people in your life, like mentors, counselors, tutors, family and friends, to help you get through, because it's difficult taking on all this alone. You need all those people in your life to help direct you when you get off course or when things get too difficult to handle.

We must utilize all resources available before we give up. Without Dr. Spearman taking the time out of his day to check on me, to see how I was doing every week, I probably wouldn't have made it through school, or even furthered my education. If it wasn't for him showing me that he cared about my education by challenging me on my decisions, I would never have continued pursuing a higher education. Having also well-rounded parents who went through some of the same challenges and issues I faced while growing up as a young man going to school, has taught me to be strong and to stay focused on my goals in life.

Watching my Mom and Dad help raise me has made me realize that, in order to make it in this world, you must have a strong support system like your family and friends to help you push through life's ups and downs. I also learned as a young man you must have God in your life to help you get through the challenges.

The special people God put in my life were the glue that helped me put the pieces together for me to succeed. Because of them, I am the person I am today. The adult influencers in my life affected my future and my choices just as much as the influence of my peers and my God. Due to God, my support system and my own diligence, I graduated in 2012 with my Bachelor of Arts Degree in Communication, with an emphasis in Marketing.

I hope and pray that one day I can take this knowledge and share it with other African Americans. Maybe someone can take my story and apply it to their life. What helped me get through all those challenges was being a believer, and faith in God.

Chapter 2

A Few Systems to Put in Place:

Working Closely with a College Counselor

by Ernest Griffin

My mentor, Mrs. Moore, really cared about her students. She always sacrificed her time to help students, like myself, with finding their way through school. Mrs. Moore set aside some time after her office hours to help students look for classes they needed for their careers and offered extra help with classes in which they struggled. She was a charismatic mentor who supported all students. Having her as my mentor was a blessing because she motivated me to want to achieve greatness in everything I did in life.

I knew that if I didn't strive for excellence in my life, I would be letting my mentor down, and I would have wasted all that time she invested in me.

I remember Mrs. Moore spent a lot of time and effort working with me, picking my classes, making sure I planned out my school week. She made sure I did all my schoolwork so that I would do well on my tests.

I remember how she always checked on me weekly to make sure I did well in all my classes and got the proper help by setting up appointments with different tutors at El Camino College. She was like a mother figure to me who gave me good advice on success.

She said, "If you want to be successful in life, you must have a plan and follow through with it, no matter the obstacles you face in life. You must stay strong and focus on what you really want out of life, because nobody is going to give it to you."

I learned to be humble from Mrs. Moore, and to always treat everyone equally, no matter who they are because no one is better than the next person, because we all have our faults and issues in life. Mrs. Moore was a short woman who came to work well dressed, with a gorgeous smile, stylish hair and classy look. Many of the students loved stopping by her office to chat with her because she was so helpful with advice on what counselor to talk to, and what career would be a good fit for students to earn a desirable, stable income. If it wasn't for Mrs. Moore setting aside time to support me, I probably wouldn't have finished junior college on time, nor qualified for a wonderful University. As a result, I went on to attend California State University Dominguez Hills (CSUDH).

Learn to Network

Networking is very important once you get to college because it leads to many opportunities to form study partners and support systems to help with one's successful progression through college.

A primary example of this is when I began my studies at California State University Dominguez Hills (CSUDH). I discovered that many of the students at this institution went to high school and junior college with me! I thought it would be wonderful to study with some of my old classmates in my university courses. This would make it easier for me to get through my classes and learn different career options. Not only was networking with familiar people important, but also learning how networking advances the outcome of one's journey through school and later in life.

My Mom and recent college professor, Mr. Smith, gave me the same advice, that networking would play a big part in my life in college and determine the outcome of my journey in life. As an adult, I learned networking is not always about *what* you know, but *who* you know.

By the time I transferred to CSUDH, I wasn't shy anymore, and my people skills had developed substantially. Due to this, I was encouraged to build new connections. I chose two people to connect with at CSUDH. Never doubt the buddy system. In college, the right buddies become your tribe. It's good to have at least one or two people you can connect and network with to help celebrate your accomplishments and support your work more effectively in subject areas you need to improve.

For example, connections at school can help you deal with homework, tests, and major projects your teacher wants you to finish within a week. I remember having two, good buddies of mine whom I connected and networked with; Clifford and Charles. Both guys played a major role in my life by helping me get through college.

I met Clifford first. He was an outstanding, very well-educated and talented brotha' from Compton, California. Clifford helped me get the books and materials I needed through his connections.

Imagine college as the Black Wall Street in Tulsa, Oklahoma, in its prime. One day, as I read about Black

Wall Street on … www.History.com … I learned that it was like the stock market is today, but was instead designed for Blacks in Tulsa, Oklahoma, between 1865 and 1920. It was built for African American people who wanted to become entrepreneurs, homeowners, and obtain loans for resources such as cars, excellent education, and other materials they needed to be successful in life. During this time, African American people had their own self-sustaining, Black economy.

After reading this I realized that, not just one person created this great economy for the Black community, but it was a group of people who came together, put their thoughts and ideas together and supported one another to create something meaning-ful.

The Black Wall Street was created to make a great impact on the African American community for years. Just like the people who created the Black Wall Street for their community, my friends and my brothers and I wanted to do the same for our community; by helping one another out for certain causes, by finishing school and obtaining good careers, and developing our best selves into becoming men of champions and giving back to our communities.

Flourishing students look out for each other by exchanging knowledge, gifts and resources. Everyone on campus knew Clifford to be outstanding and talented. He was involved in many activities at school like Drama Club, Hip-Hop Group, and the African American Social Club. CJ, as we called him, knew how to rap and write well, and always battled with other rappers in the student hall. With Clifford so involved in many different programs and activities on campus, I was able to connect and network with *his connections.*

And then there's my good friend, Charles. He also helped me get through school. Who would have guessed that Charles would become one of my longtime friends as well? He was a very talented and skilled brotha', involved in many different things, from sports, fashion, entertainment, and education. I met Charles while taking an English class and soon developed a friendship well beyond.

I really didn't know Charles was involved in a lot of stuff until the end of the semester. We were paired together for our final group project of the year. We had to get together and come up with a good news story. We both decided to come up with a sports story about Kobe Bryant and the Lakers trying to make their way back to into yet another championship.

Charles knew some people who worked in the sport entertainment world, and asked a few different industry people about the Lakers organization and how Kobe could get them back on top. After a week of research, Charles and I got all the information together that we needed about Kobe and the Lakers and we wrote the best, most interesting story. This resulted in both of us receiving good grades in class. If it wasn't for Charles' connections and networking with those he knew, we would never have gotten the information to write this great story about Kobe and the Lakers.

Charles didn't just help me get through some of my classes; he also helped me get my first, much-needed intern job in order to complete my credits toward graduation. The intern gig was at the KJLH radio station in Inglewood, California.

While there, I networked with different people in the music industry and learned about being a disc jockey, marketing, and giving back to the community. Being a DJ, I learned you must have people skills, know your music, how to market, understand the importance of giving back to the community, and be very animated because when you're on the radio, sometimes you have to quickly switch into different characters to reach out to various types of people.

Clifford and Charles helped me get through a lot by helping me build relationships with other, like-minded people. Throughout college, I learned that networking with just one or two people, doors opened for me, which led to new opportunities toward reaching my goals. These are things I would never have been able to do all alone. You never know when someone's value will become a resource toward your own. Everyone has something to contribute. Networking with individuals and different groups, can help you achieve success in all aspects of life.

Stay Focused on Your Goals

Staying focused on my goals was a priority even while in college. I continued to stay connected with positive people, which helped to motivate and inspire me. My goals were to finish school with decent grades, retain the materials I learned in my classes and make sure I set a foundation for a good career.

While I was still at El Camino, I met with a counselor and teacher by the name of Mr. Russo. Mr. Russo taught Public Relations (PR) classes in the Communications Department. He was someone who desired the best for everyone and gave us all the proper help we needed. An outstanding counselor, he made sure I understood what I needed to do in order to make it through my classes.

I remember when I first met with Mr. Russo. I told him my goals, whereupon he looked at me and said, "Well, it's up to you how successful you want to be, because nobody's surely going to give it to you. You have to want it."

He continued, "By getting good grades, you have to work hard and work long nights in order to get the grades you want." Mr. Russo set up a plan for me to set up my classes. While getting those classes set up, I had to set aside a study schedule to make sure I finished all my work on time.

Mr. Russo made sure I understood the importance of this and to use that knowledge to the best of my ability to succeed in school and in life. Through all my training and preparation, I learned that staying dedicated to my present tasks and focusing on my goals, helped me to become successful.

By the time I finished at Cal-State Dominguez Hills, I already had a good career working for Hertz Car Rental, which was the #1 rental company in the industry. I started at the bottom and worked my way up to become a manager. This wouldn't have been possible had I not stayed focused in school by completing my classes and getting the extra help I needed from all my assets.

Although I had my good friends, CJ, Charles, Dr. Spearman, Mrs. Moore, and Mr. Russo helping me in life, I also had my family (whom I love, dearly) helping to raise and guide me through my young, adult life. Like my Mother used to say to me, "It takes a village to raise a boy into a man." As I got older, I definitely understood what my Mom meant.

It's important to remember who helped raise us and helped got us through the tribulations of life. My journey was definitely a long one, but without the support and foundation of my mentors, teachers, family and friends, I wouldn't have made it very far without them.

Despite what I went through, I never let it defeat me. Remember, you may experience daily struggles, but don't forget that you too can have a great support system. Your support team can be your blood family or your social group. You can always make the decision to have a blessed circle of support. Just don't forget who they are as you mature into your destiny.

Chapter 3

There Are No Coincidences
Or Ironies

By Phorode Brown

There are no coincidences or ironies.
God is present in every situation,
During every moment
And through every obstacle.

Going off to college was one of the most exciting times of my life. I got the opportunity to experience the world as a young adult, making my own decisions and mistakes, while learning from them both. I met a small world of diverse people with different personalities; some of which became lifelong friends. Through it all, I learned that no matter who we encounter, how many times we fall short and how many accomplishments we achieve, the greatest moments of learning can only be taught through our life experiences. Our own individual walk in life always has a way of revealing that there is, indeed, a power far greater than us.

The older we get and the more is exposed to us, we each tend to let some things go, whereupon we gravitate toward new things, new people and places. At some point purposely, our wants and desires become uncontrollable, and before we know it our lives are out of balance. At such times, we don't have any idea of what's real and, while we're at a standstill as the world spins, we forget that God is supposed to be guiding our footsteps.

Let's examine our journey with God as that of a child with their parent on a trip to the grocery store; God (being the parent) and us (as the child). With thoughts fixated on everything *we want*, we dash about the aisles of life forgetting that we didn't come to the store alone. We came with God! He knows the store better than we do and we're supposed to be led by him. Without guidance, we are very liable to letting our eyes be greater than our stomachs, while we pull down all those things off the shelves of life, into a pile of mess on the floor. Then, we take things we cannot pay for, or worse, get lost in a world of 'things' we know nothing about.

It's important to seek God's guidance in all situations. How many of us are like the child in the grocery store? I admit that, like the petulant child, I stepped out into this world without necessarily following the guidance of God, my leader. Although obstacles blocked my path along my journey, God was still with me.

As I matriculated through college, I faced countless obstacles and hardships. I was even placed in handcuffs for the first time in my life. Every hurdle presented me with the reassurance that I was not in total control of things, nor the way they played out.

When I think about it now, I know there was an unseen force looking out for my greater good. Something, or someone guiding me, made sure that even though I stumbled, I didn't fall. Like most people looking for understanding, I began to acknowledge God in more situations and eventually came to understand two things.

The first is that, as we walk this journey of life, we're going to be tried and tested to fulfill our purpose. The second is that, while fulfilling our purpose, none of us should walk this walk alone; not only to serve God but to become the greatest versions of ourselves in the process of 'our becoming.'

By fulfilling our purpose in that which we've been called to do, we allow ourselves to grow into a more complete version of who, and what we believe, we are. We begin by living and acting *with purpose* and that we cultivate the drive to seek out and create change! For example, I feel my purpose in life is to inspire and motivate people through their own experiences to reach their next level. I use my own experiences to do the same.

With every person I encounter, my purpose is to leave that experience with them, to motivate and inspire them to live through their purpose. That is always my intention. That is always my objective.

During this journey or process, we are faced with experiences that are meant to strengthen us. Every day, God presents to us a moment where our will, faith and discernment are meant to be exercised. It's also our responsibility to understand and grasp that none of this can be done or obtained *without God*. To make sure that the things I was asking God to do and change in my life weren't in vain, I had to begin moving in the direction of the things I sought.

For instance, I wanted and asked for a better relationship with my son; the kind I didn't have with my father when I was a young man. I wanted my son to be able to talk to me about anything and express himself to me at times when he felt like no one else in this world was listening. I wanted to be his role model, and for him to look up to me as someone he wanted to be just like, if not better than.

In return, I had to make myself available to those things. Hence, I began to work on the relationship with my son, to understand him and become his voice of reason and love, instead of anger and miscommunication, which is how we can be sometimes as parents and adults.

I had to trust that God would direct my footsteps and I soon began to see those things manifest in my life. My son began talking to me about random things he was curious about as a young teenager and young man. In his own way, he began to act like me, picking up certain phrases or mannerisms that he saw in me.

Once I began to see the things I trusted God to align and prepare for me, the more confidence and clarity I harnessed to step into my purpose. God gave me more opportunities to grow into something more eminent, more opportunities to motivate and inspire people. It was in those moments that I displayed and exercised those principles, disciplines and discernments that God, indeed, instilled within me. I had to trust the process.

As stated earlier, at every stage in life there are experiences we must go through, designed to help us get to our next level. Resources are provided to us to help us along the way. My resources in college came in the form of several helping hands and foreseeing eyes; from people who had visions of me beyond what

I saw for myself. Imagine skipping class with a few friends one day (something harmless we can all possibly relate too), only to end up in handcuffs! Then, being placed in the back of a police car for the very first time in your life, not knowing the outcome of the situation that caused you to get there.

I didn't take my college experience too seriously early on. This was my first real experience being away from home and my family. There was this new sense of freedom where I didn't have anyone telling me what to do, what to wear or what time to get up. For the first time, I was making decisions on my own.

On this particular day, I made the decision to skip class and get high with my friends. What started out as *harmless, young adult fun,* quickly turned into me almost losing my chance at an education! More importantly, my freedom as a young man was seriously jeopardized. Even though I came out of that situation a better person, the thought of what could have happened have always stuck with me.

I can only speak for myself and say that God put me in that situation in order to push me to change. I put my education at risk, I took a chance on my freedom and could have thrown my entire life away *in one moment,* but God proved that he was right there walking with me, like any other time in my life. I take full accountability for my actions and decisions in that situation. If God hadn't used me in that situation, I would never have been able to see that I had to be *more aware* of who and what I was influenced by, I honestly don't know where I would be today.

The impact those influences could have had on my life down the line, may have been much more severe. The worst part wasn't the 'getting in trouble.' While I was sitting in the back of the police car, the professor whose class I skipped, saw me. She walked by the car and there was a moment where we just stared at each other. I had a look of embarrassment, but hers was a look of disappointment. That's what hurt more than anything.

When we respect someone or think highly of them, their opinion and perception of us matters! I then realized I had not been living up to the potential God allowed others to see in me. When I truly began to change, the things and people around me changed as well.

When I finally got a chance to speak with that same professor, she asked me three questions that have always stuck with me until today. "If you are what you do, then what does it mean when others make the decision for you?" … and … "How well do you truly understand what you're doing and why, as you're actually doing it?" I didn't come to understand the importance of these questions as they were presented to me right then, but as I went through life, they grew to become more meaningful. Since this conversation, I learned to allow God to lead my steps. I graduated from college with my Bachelor of Science Degree in Child and Family Development.

My primary focus today is to motivate and inspire, not only those in my communities, but also across the world. I strive to bring about social change to our neighborhoods and communities. If life is indeed about change, then why not start in our own backyards? In our communities, too many of our young children are locked out of opportunities.

It's my goal to recover the key and unlock those doors for those who wish to join the walk with others who have been called to fulfill a higher purpose. I must start first by working toward becoming the greatest version of myself every day, while acknowledging and being aware that someone is always watching me; whether waiting for me to stumble and fall or being the reason why someone never gave up.

I leave you with this: no matter the amount of degrees, achievements, promotions or setbacks, your reach, your impact must be greater than them all. For what good is it to be a man who opens doors, when we don't allow others to walk through them, alongside him? You were inspired by the world; allow the world to be inspired by you.

First, make sure that you are around positive people, and those who look for growth. Learn from other people's experiences, as well as their own. This way, you may bring awareness about your experiences as an African American.

Second, we must begin doing the work necessary to bring change to our communities. God encourages us to have *the courage* to change our communities. We have a responsibility to bring forth that change.

Last, but certainly not least, build and cultivate a relationship with God to understand why certain things happen in our lives.

Chapter 4

Steps to Succeed in College

by Phorode Brown

To support African American men, I believe we must first create awareness. Sharing with other African American men our struggles, goals and achievements is a release.

African American men need to know and share their perspectives and views on what it's like *to be*. We must know who the people are that believe in us, whose opinions we value, what we see and what we wish to see; versus what we see in ourselves. This is what matters most. Being aware is not only about problems and flaws that we see in others but recognizing the ones that are within ourselves as well.

We can do this by conducting community meetings with the mature men and younger men in our communities, while orchestrating discussion panels and groups. It's detrimental to our future generations that we begin to build trusting relationships. This can also be achieved outside of formal meetings. When was the last time you knocked on your brother's door to talk about things you could do to uplift your neighborhood?

We must begin doing the work needed to bring change to our communities. Our men should know the power of service, the essence of giving back, and the true understanding that we cannot continue to abundantly *take* from our communities and scarcely ever *give back* to them. Life doesn't work like that. God doesn't work like that!

Teach what you learn and have the courage to apply it. When we find out what works in our communities, we must reach out to other men in *other communities* and share what we learned, and what works. We are too well connected, whether it via be social media, our jobs, churches, local pickup games at the park, even our schools. It doesn't matter. We have to reach out and truly communicate with one another.

Bad news spreads quickly, but if we took that same energy and applied it to where we need it most in our lives, in positive ways, then the possibilities of what we could do together are endless.

Like everything around us, change is inevitable. It's a situation that's unavoidable. American motivational speaker, author, radio DJ, former TV host and politician, Les Brown, says in a video, from which I paraphrase, "Either we make a move on life, or life will be forced to move on us."

Developmental change! Because it gives you a chance to recognize that you are not the same person you were yesterday or last week. You are not the same person you were last month or last year! It's critical that you scrutinize your life, daily. Self-reflect and begin to change bad habits and behaviors that could potentially slow down or hinder your progress toward being the greatest version of yourself. It's necessary! The more you change, the more your environment changes.

This does not mean that you won't struggle. It doesn't mean you won't experience heartache or failure. No! These are necessary for your growth. What it does mean is that your judgment about your present and future self will become unmoved by negative influences. Not all, but most.

Your confidence and trust in your talents, skills and abilities won't be shaken easily by competition or envy. The more confidence you allow to show forth from what God created you to be (before you were blinded by the social constructs of everyday life), the less discouraged the world can make you feel, as you break through your social conditioning and return to your natural self.

Relationships shape and mold our viewpoints on life. How we act and react to people daily reflects how we feel about ourselves. Most people who experience an abundance of love throughout their lives will essentially meet and greet others in a loving manner.

Dually, people who don't experience this love in some cases are more distant or bordered. They may long for a meaningful and loving relationship, but may not know how to express it. To know love *is to be love.*

What love is greater than God's love?

A relationship with God is important because, ultimately, He is your life-partner. Particularly, when he shows up in the form of a significant other, our families, our children. It's the love we have for our cohorts and the people in our neighborhoods and communities.

Having a relationship with God is the only way to truly experience the power of his love and grace. In experiencing this, I've learned that love is on our side. God is love.

Chapter 5

Experiencing Racism in College

By Dr. Emanuel Officer

Walk with me as I give you an implicit look that vacillates between the truth and lies. This myopic view always pivots within the frame of reality.

'Micro-aggression, passive aggression, support-less, stereotypes, isolated, seclusion'---these are just a few words that I heard two, Emerson College, African American male students say in March of 2015.

As I listened to these young men, I heard the frustration in their voices as they continued talking about their experiences in college. This is a quote from these two, young, African American men, as follows:

"I don't feel supported in college. I'm expected to be enrolled in prison, rather than college. I'm mistreated whenever I'm in school. People walk around me to avoid me at all cost. They make no eye contact; they immediately feel uncomfortable, shy, scared-faced. They stereotype me into the criminal thug, brooding gangbanger. Black men with hoodies are avoided as though the hood defines the content of my character.

They avoid me, yet they are surprised to see that I'm exactly the opposite of what they expected, neither Whites, nor Blacks. So, because I choose to stay to myself and be by myself, I'm immediately made into an outcast in a world where I cannot benefit.

Where can I find support in the place that tries to belittle me and take advantage of me? From a Black and White community, it's bad that our school is less than 3% Black, and at least 70% White. Now, I must deal with ignorant bigots screaming the N-word from their cars. I have to deal with White girls and their insecurities; learned behavior taught to fear me at the first look. To deal with the overt racism, micro-aggression, stereotypes, passive-aggressive kids, and personalities who honestly give no thought of me, (and a place where I'm not supported).

I'm discouraged to do the things I want to. I sometimes feel oppressed. College begins to feel like a prison, and I'm in a holding cell waiting to be put on death row."

The two students described micro-aggression as: verbal behavior, hostility, and racial slights only directed toward Black students on this particular campus. The passive-aggression they described, indicated that White students had the same aggression, but in a passive way. For example, a passive-aggressive statement commonly used is, "You people are so aggressive."

As I reflect on the experience these two students expressed, I agree with their perspective. We, as Black men, live in a world that revolves in a matrix wherein every time we reach the status quo, the goalpost is moved. You can meet all the standards and qualifications and follow the criteria to the letter, but somehow, they just can't get past you being Black in America.

Now, this is a taboo subject. Whenever you hear the words, 'You're pulling the race card," you automatically know you're dealing with a racist. In principle, this means relating to the ideal that one must not identify with varying circumstances. There should never be any respective person. Everyone must meet the same criteria, but that's not the case for young Black men. The two most important things in the world are information and communication. Information and communication are the backbone for observation and explanation. Time will not wait, nor respect your choice as a prerequisite between the time you make it, and the course in which your choice is carried out. In other words: time waits for *No One*.

If you show up in class for a test you didn't study for, it's too late to get that time back. It's gone. Your cooperation was required ahead of time! Knowledge is power.

Understanding is the power toward freedom. You have to look at the American college institutions as rocks that are never going to move when you push them. Rather, you must learn how to be strengthened by them. You have got to get ahead of the goalposts by *forecasting* and *focusing* like a *think tank!* With these concepts in mind, I've discovered my calling in life. I was not always a doctor. I'm a native of Indianapolis, Indiana, and I didn't always like school, but I learned to love being taught and to teach others. I'm a Christian existentialist. I also stand firm on the belief that when one thinks one knows everything, one no longer has the ability to learn *anything!* A lesson that can't be taught is a lesson that can't be learned. My existential beliefs have been adopted from Immanuel Kant, and my former professor, Dr. Willie J. Duncan, who was voted by Oxford University as one of the most intellectual minds of the 21st century, with his *Theory of One*. My moral belief is that the mind has incorporeal perceptual probability; that there is a truth outside the explanation and observational truth that is unseen, untapped and undiscovered. It's simply an unrelated thought. Ideas create ideas, and creation creates creation.

So, what you think was---isn't. And what you thought wasn't---is.

As an educator, my approach is to take truth beyond a boombasteration (i.e., an agglomeration of artificial language) of multiple articulations that set up another tautological (i.e., circles) argument, with no resolve. I want to sow seeds of knowledge that produce crops of teachers and leaders who exemplify skills that can teach in any arena in the world.

I use the term "existential" from the philosopher, Immanuel Kant, who dealt with categorical imperatives, which is a moral obligation that's binding in every point. I use this word to explain moral laws and ethics for all ethnicities, not just Whites.

Boombasteration: the root word 'bombastic'—means: inflated, a bunch of air, not meaning much.

Agglomeration---means: a group of things put into categories, in or out of order.

After successfully completing college and graduate school, I encourage you to remember your mission in life. Your mission must also be beyond the accepted standard. Every vision must have a *prevision*, and every standard requires a demanding criterion and a premise.

The premise of the promise depends on you meeting the standards and qualifications. There is a vibrant, radiating pulse in the atmosphere with the elusive reality that looks like something you can't see and feel. Like something you can't touch, but it's yours---right now!---if you want it by faith.

It doesn't matter what obstacles block your way. Just go around it! Do what is required of you by God. YOU must go through it.

Life is the teacher. Within every expectation is an experience toward finding yourself. It's an inward journey that only *you* can start. It's the dominant thoughts of our lives that direct our paths. Do you know your path? Do you know your purpose?

Or, are you waiting on someone else's affirmation and validation that may 'subliminally' suggest who you are? You can't allow one drop of negativity to infiltrate your mind-growth. The predictability of complex systems, the slightest change, the smallest move can alter your mind-growth elevation.

There is no set schedule for variations in orientations when you allow your mind-growth to be interrupted. In order for our minds to block this interruption, it's imperative that we, as African American men, remember a few concepts.

First, focus and time management are key to personal and professional skills that lead to success in life. Second, acknowledge personal fears. Lastly, keep dreaming and never allow anyone or anything to stop you from pursuing those dreams.

Chapter 6

Key Concepts to Remember

By Dr. Emanuel Officer

When I was in middle school and high school, I was placed into Special Education. I was bused from the city all the way to the suburbs, where the school curriculum was more challenging. I remember a kid asked me to spell the word 'lunch box.' I had a lunch box in my hand with the word 'lunch box' written on it, but because I didn't take the time to look and read it, I was embarrassed because I couldn't spell it.

I was determined to take my mind to higher learning. Everything in high school for me was advanced, so it made me work harder to keep up. The curriculum didn't wait for me; I had to catch up to the curriculum. In this age of cell phones and computers, kids have much more access to finding new definitions and research. It's a push button away. If I can light a candle and read a book, surely, with the new technology they have at their disposal, they can take their minds to higher learning.

One of the biggest problems in colleges is that students can't read. If we keep giving them the A B C's and nothing else, they will have a fixed mindset that's not subject to change. There will be no growth, reform, change, or security. I know that a lesson that can't be taught, is a lesson that can't be learned, but in this age of moving the goal post, Black students must become 'think tanks'.

Become students who study and show themselves approved; workmen who need not be ashamed, like I was! I don't want it to be easy. I want them to seek knowledge so they can rightly identify truth. When they speak, their syntax and diction should be clearly expressed how they intend it to be received rhetorically, before their audience, with masterful phraseology and oral articulation.

Focus and Time Management

The greatest waste of time is---something you have no time for. The greatest waste of time is---something you said 'yes' to, but should've said 'no'. Instead, focus and forecast. Think of the things you don't have time for, in comparison to things you said 'yes' to; and things you think you should've said 'no' to. As you reflect on this, remember that self-discovery is sometimes a violent, penetrating act. It's better for you to find out now rather than spend a lifetime running back to the drawing board of life.

You have to be honest with yourself. Admit, submit, then commit to yourself. Explore the options of truth. The secularization of American institutions should not change your rational and thinking. You have to remain diligent and forthright in finishing your work.

You can't allow lethargic, hard-to-raise conscious thinking, and willful ignorance to reroute your path. Stop worrying about something you can't do anything about. Change who you are from the inside out. Then change the world. You can't tie an ox to an ass: one is lazy and stubborn, while the other is hard-working. One is connected; the other is disconnected. You can't dress up a male pig in a white suit; when you let him out the door, he'll going straight to the mud pit.

Why? Because that is his nature. When you know the nature of a thing, why do you look at it as though some strange thing has happened? Some people resolve their reality by not meeting their expectations. They turn on the failsafe switch by accepting the lesser accomplishments as their real**ity,** rather than acknowledging their unrealized reality failed to be discovered because of their need for "safety."

Lethargic: to be sluggish or lazy.

You must remain diligent and forthright in finishing your work. You can't allow lethargic, hard-to-raise conscious thinking and willful ignorance reroute your path. Everybody knows the elephant is in the room, but racism refuses to explore the options of truth.

The only way you're going to get your life off 'pause' and back on 'play' is through focus and time management. Focus—something we find hard to do in our day-to-day life, when we have too much on our plate.

We are shipwrecked and rerouted and taken through the maze of life. We must commit to, and move forward toward, only that which we submit to in our daily activities. You must ask yourself, "What can I do to provide my greatest impact? Where is my focus?"

Managing time better will lead to places of *knowledge*. This is not a question of knowing; it's an answer of time management. Limits exist within the effectiveness of time management.

When you understand your value, you cultivate your effectiveness, and you won't have to live your life under someone else's approval. Don't rush, take your time and get what you need, because the value is in what YOU need.

The difference between effectiveness and failure depends on what YOU need, and your courage to grasp whatever that is! You need today's experience to get to tomorrow's expectations.

Let your effectiveness eliminate everything that has no value. When you understand your value, growth, reform, and change outgrow what you don't need. Understanding the information should give you the comprehension.

There will be times when you are physically and mentally drained, but everything you do in the direction of your goal, no matter how big or small, will be effective in your quest.

Don't give your energy away to things that have no meaning. Give your power to the prominent things. There has never been a fresh, innovative idea on the horizon that didn't take a fight or go through a struggle.

Every reality was once a dream; a master plan that came to fruition. Every possibility becomes possible when you remove it from an unrelated thought. They said it couldn't be done; they found it could be. They said it didn't exist, but they found it, anyway. Don't build your comprehension structure on entities that cannot invest in you. The quest toward the power of freedom is believing in one's self. If you don't believe in you, you can't convince anyone else to do so.

Every working entity has an operating and systematic order that must be followed. Your structure must have its own autonomy, not always derived from a self-serving, sufficient governing body or blind institution. If you can't see it and can't hear it, you won't believe it.

You will never know how good it feels to get up, until you stand up on your own two feet! Once you've been a slave and set free, you'll never be a slave again! Your ideas will create ideas in your creation, and your creation will create creations.

You'll become an innovative, outside-the-box thinker; no longer subjected to meager, embryonic, surface understanding.

If you've never been set free, and remain a slave, you will never understand the power of freedom, which is the experience of understanding. Don't waste any time or effort on an entity that disparages a system---that you know works! You are your own investment, so you have to make sure you have enough operating capital.

Why are you waiting for your pay off?

Marianne Williamson (1992) once said, "Our deepest fear is not that we are inadequate. Our deepest fear is that we are powerful beyond measure." (p.125).

We ask ourselves, "Who are we? Are we brilliant, handsome, talented, fabulous?" The bigger question is, "Who are you *not to be*?" Only you can bring out who you were truly meant to be. Don't let anyone's validation subliminally suggest who you are. The real you screams to be unleashed and become that which you don't even realize you are yet. So, who will you be today? Will you be weak, bruised, battered, beaten, defeated? Or triumphant, powerful, victorious and resoundingly unequivocal?

Considering how big you are, it might frighten you to realize how small you are, in your present state of comfort. Another man's rhetoric is just misplaced information. It's past tense. Therefore, his rhetoric is saying a lot of things, but doing nothing. 'Hearers and sayers' only *talk* about doing.

Remember this: negativity and lies will always follow positivity and truth. When you plant a good seed, negativity is right there, waiting to plant a bad seed. Its job is to challenge and question, and attempt to usurp the authority of truth. It wants to grow along with the truth you planted and choke the life out of it. It wants to keep the matrix pulled over the eyes of success. It wants the dreamer to give up, get out, and believe there is no hope, convinced that 'life can't work.' It wants you to believe you're wasting your time as it waits in the waning shadows along the narrow path of life, making certain that the *best you* is afraid to come out into the light!

Negativity will have you chanting antics out of the waning shadows! Stop living in a dream. Step into your new horizon and don't look back at twilight. There are dirty, dark, dusty places beckoning for you to remain when opportunity is knocking at the door. Don't let DELAY Be your most deadly form of denial!

Procrastination will steal anything that you don't cease. Understand and know when opportunity is knocking at your door. Don't waste any time and energy on failure because it's not cost effective. Failure will infect you with its venom and poison that can reach and spread like a plague.

Negative words sink under your skin and poison the heart, giving you negative thoughts. Negative thoughts will give you negative emotions; negative emotions will give you negative circumstances; and negative circumstances will have you making negative choices. Just replace positives where negatives are. Recognize a 'yes' and give it your time and energy. You are your sustaining capital.

The easiest thing in the world to do is to give up. The hardest thing in the world to do is to try again, and again. I'm not talking about saying, "I'm going to attempt to try." Just because you tried one or two times doesn't mean that you really tried.

Trying is attempting, over and over until you accomplish your goal. You add some here, take some out there, and you get all the components you need for your victory.

To be successful, you have to find the driving force in you and tap into it, understand it, know it, master it and then put it into operation. That is the only way that you will access and expose the fire in you, to accomplish your education, graduate with the degree of your desire, and beyond.

Anything with a foundation and structure did not happen quickly; it took time, effort and study to make it work. Some people are so knowledge-driven that they are driving dumb.

Its ignorance perpetrates brilliance but is nothing more than a 'boombasteration' of multiple articulations that bring up another tautological argument, and ugly agglomeration of misplaced things.

Above all, *focus* is the main objective!

Remember: information communication, observation, explanation, and isolation elevation. If you break the cycle, you change the choice. Choices are nothing but cycles that need to be broken. Focusing and time management will keep you alert, and you won't be distracted and caught off guard. One great method of motivation is motivating yourself: stand in the mirror and tell yourself what you're going to accomplish.

Tell yourself what you're going to cut loose. Lay aside every weight and strip those things that beset you far too easily, and set you back. Disconnect from every person, place, and thing that does not cultivate and correlate with your reality.

Look yourself in the eyes and tell yourself, "I'm not going to let you stop me from accomplishing my goals." Great ideas and concepts don't need to be sold. The solution sells itself; therefore, sell yourself! You are your greatest asset; you are your greatest commodity. No matter what it is, how great or how small, reach high and don't settle for the scraps and rotten apples.

Fear.

Fear will have you addicted to failure, inferiority and uncertainty. This ambiguity cares nothing about your failure in the process. In fact, your cooperation is not even a prerequisite of your understanding on this. Fear will keep you on the emotional roller coasters of life, running like a hamster on the treadmill going nowhere, locked in a cage with a created climate and atmosphere that becomes normal.

You think you are the victim, but you really are the predator because you have decided to stay afraid and do nothing about where you are. You have allowed failure to interrupt the flow of your success. It's an open door to let any other disruption in. One thing opens the door to another.

Fear changes and challenges one's belief system. Fear usually results in insults and apprehension because being wrong (allegedly) made you a failure, but being wrong should be celebrated, because it means you have been elevated to true mind-growth and true understanding!

Your mind must be open to true and new understandings, even if it threatens the current belief systems, in order to enhance your identity toward true reality. Rhetoric and lies have conditioned the mind to insanity, paralyzing the heart to keep the body still. God provided us with an opportunity for wealth and he's not going to spoon-feed or force you to drink it.

If you believe in yourself, someone else will believe in what you represent. Remember, understanding your value will cultivate your effectiveness.

Put together a think tank. If it's our classmates who think like you do in higher learning, make sure every component works together as one unit. Talk about the issues that go on around the campus. You will never overcome something that you don't conquer.

Giving up is not an option. If you have the proper mechanics, with the right components, your order will never be breached. When the mechanics have been breached, you'll be faced with hierarchy and provocation.

Enhance, and then re-enhance; this is your structure. Willful ignorance will never explore the options of truth. Life will beat the purpose out of you. Fear will keep you in corporate slavery. Fear will make sure you fail.

You have to adapt to being Black in America; as doctors, lawyers, judges, senators, governors and mayors. Whatever your discipline in America, you're going to have to deal with racism.

It's an inescapable plight. You have to take what you have and use it to the fullest extent. Give up any person, place or thing challenging your dream; cut them loose! What saves you? Is it you jumping into the net waiting below?

If you don't know how to swim, what saves you? Is it the hand reaching from the boat, or you reaching to the hand? You have to take what you have and use it. Whatever does not serve your vision, cut it loose!

People will lack faith and enthusiasm for your vision if you yourself do not believe in it. Surround yourself with successful people. Be ferocious and go for yours with tenacity, conviction, and authority. But don't jump without preparation and the right tools. You want to make sure you land in the right position in life. Always have contingency plans.

Don't invest your time, money, or energy on any dead ideas that keep you running back to the drawing board of life. Your time is one of your most precious, treasured commodities, and you can't afford to squander it away.

If that investment is in the wrong place, get it back. Time will not wait, nor respect your choices, nor bother to see if your course is carried out. Remember, life is the teacher and every expectation is an experience toward finding yourself. Don't settle for a season and missed expectations.

Never let desperation enter your cipher. It will keep you spinning your wheels in the mud and you'll keep adding the water. The hunger of desperation will have you eating anything in the house while you've missed the table that's already been spread for you.

Assess and identify yourself with persons, places and things that cultivate and identify your reality. In the seven liberal arts, the word, 'liberate,' came from the Latin word, 'liber,' meaning, 'set free.' If you educate your mind, you're no longer a slave to ignorance. It's the dominant thoughts of your life that will direct the path of your destiny.

Commit to a solution that works for you. Let your perseverance and passion be the driving force in your life. Life is a mystery if you have no understanding. Success and brilliance are waiting to be released from you. Don't walk away from the mirror and forget who you are. Let the true reflections come out in excess and expose your talent, intellect, and gifts.

Don't let the paralysis of fear give you a prognosis of nonverbal, inactive, lethargic, insecurity and paranoia. Get off the respirator and plug into the life-support that is increased in your character and feel YOUR pulse. Know that you're not brain-dead. Don't let the poison of self-deception destroy your belief system. Use every exegetical tool to change the world.

Keep Dreaming.

I had a dream that I was back home in Indianapolis, Indiana, at 2040 West Coyle Street. On the edge of Knowlton Road, was a house of my childhood friends. I noticed there was a big beautiful door on the house that wasn't there before. The door was so beautiful, it changed the whole look of the house, like a mansion.

Still in the dream, I saw one of my childhood friends, and I said to her, "The door on your house is beautiful. It changes the whole look, like your house is brand-new." She replied, "Emanuel, that door has always been there."

There are doors of racism, bigotry, profiling, jealousy, anger and insecurity that will shut in your face. But don't worry; turn the knob and walk into a new situation. Or turn the knob and walk out of a bad one. Just because the doors close does not mean there is not a new door in your life that's open.

The negatives in life are the darkness that show us the light which developed and evolved into what shines brightest. You'll have to be exposed to all kinds of lights to penetrate that darkness. In the end, you will have plenty of positive exposures to give you a clear picture on life, on yourself, on God' purpose for you.

Don't let the dream killers and vision assassins kill you, dreaming out loud with your eyes wide open while still not being able to wake up. You have to counter-maneuver and outflank the fiery darts that racism is going to shoot at you. You have to have an evasive plan to move ahead of the goalposts. Go beyond the constraints and barriers of traditional rules and be better than good; be better than excellent; be better than superb.

Be you! Get an overhead view of the maze that was set up to block you in. Know every exit so you'll never be trapped.

Do something every day that drives you in the direction of your goal, and you will find yourself in a wealthy place. Where there is no dream or vision, the people perish. Don't let your dreams be just a fading shadow and echo dissipating in the thunder, in a moment of time. Use your greatest asset---your brain.

Be a great thinker; be innovative. Allow your mind to change phenomena. That truly is the power of your freedom for any barrier, pothole and curve that shows up on your path. Remember again, that knowledge is power. The power in freedom is understanding.

Chapter 7

Vessels of Strength, Prayer, And The Covering

By Amber N. Hearn, DMFT
Ernest Griffin, B.A.
Phorode Brown, B.S.
Emanuel Officer, Ph.D.

Reader, we are happy that you made it
to this chapter so that we can commune
with you in prayer.

Turn the page and let us now pray for you ...

Our Father, who art in heaven, holy is YOUR name, dear God.

Lord, we ask you to cover and protect each person reading this book, and all the Vessels of Strength in YOUR eyes.

Please help their eyes to see whom you have called them to be and whom you sent into their lives to support, guide and help them move into the purpose you ordained for them.

Help them to have the courage and wisdom to never fear when obstacles come their way.

Lord, help the readers' goals to line up with your goals, Lord, and let time management be a part of their daily lives.

Lord, let your light shine before men, that they may see your good works and glorify your Father, which is in heaven.

In Jesus' Name, Amen.

Please know that God is here to support you always. We also extend our support to you as mentors in Christ.

We speak healing of past hurts in your lives; as well as prosperity, confidence, courage, focus, time management and a closer relationship with God, and knowing how to be effective in your connection with the people that God sends into your life.

For prayer and/or words of encouragement, please connect with us by e-mail at:

vesselsofstrength@gmail.com

As we continue to pray for you, we want to cover you with words of wisdom and encouragement through "The Covering" by the father-mentor at *Vessels of Strength*: Dr. Emanuel Officer, on the next page …

The Covering

By Dr. Emanuel Officer

This section raises issues concerning the lies and deception resulting from racism, and encourages you to never believe them. In fact, the covering encourages you to believe in your *own truth* about yourself and disregard the pseudo statements about who you are.

Do Not Believe the Lies and Deception!

Vladimir Lenin said, "A lie told often enough becomes the truth." My college professor once said, "Lies are started by the enemy, spread through ignorance and accepted by fools without inquiry."

Liars have to balance and equate their story with other lies. Lies cannot give us real choices and evidence, from real observation, because polarity pulls from every side. One side *demands* while the other side *commands*. The lie can never receive closure because its evaluation is yet another aberration or fluctuation from the truth. The more you hold liars to the truth, the angrier they get.

The truth either proves the fact---or not. The world's system is a reflection of images hidden inside a matrix circumfused as reality. The lie is 'smoke and mirror' images, bouncing off other lies to throw the scent off the dogs, allowing the liar can flourish.

The truth now falls on death because all it can see is *skin color*. The newest lie is called 'alternative fact'. Now, it's either a lie or the truth. The truth, on the other hand, is one or many facts leading to the truth. It can be *one* fact (i.e. truth viewed ten different ways, but is still one fact). The only way a lie can be a fact, is if it is, in fact, a lie.

Alternative facts are not even an artificial language, which usually removes the ambiguity to cause an exhaustive range of arguments.

On the contrary, IT'S JUST ANOTHER LIE!

Deception is created to perpetuate social, economic, environmental and cultural injustice that's in the DNA of racism.

Are we still one nation under God? With liberty and justice for all? Or, are we living in two Americas? As long as there are *alternative facts*, which is the new caveat of incendiary bootstrapping nonsense, it will keep hatred alive and America divisive.

While racism still exists, you do not have to be governed by it. Remember, you can accomplish whatever you put your mind to, despite inevitable challenges. Always know who you are and what your true purpose in life is. NO ALTERNATIVE FACT about YOU is a fact. The lie about you becomes true when you believe it!

When you know who you are, No One can tell you who you are. God is encouraging you to not only KNOW who you are, but also to know who you are NOT. YOU are NOT inferior from others; YOU are NOT Ignorant; YOU are NOT Poor; YOU are NOT ineffective; and YOU are NOT a failure! Remember, your elevation in life begins with your mind.

Wake Up!

I woke up this morning thanking God, first, for another day and I prayed, as always. After turning off the audio Bible, which I listen to every night, my mind began to wonder about all the stories I've read; all the documentaries I've watched, the marches I've seen and speeches I've heard. And I've come to the conclusion that no portfolio or dossier exists canonizing our history, that has not been altered, obfuscated and covered up by egregious, mendacious nocuous, maniacal pseudo.

We are expected to live off the success of the 1960s, but this is 2019. We have to *Wake Up!* and find another way around the roadblocks of institutional, instruct-

racism in the DNA of America. And, this is not going anywhere soon! We have to start a new chapter, build a new biography with accountability for today and for the future of our children---not written by someone else. We must educate their minds to deal with the reality around them.

We have to stop the brainwashing and reprogram their minds to focus on an objective state, and bring out the brilliance of young, Black world-changers! Knowledge is power, but understanding is the power to freedom. No longer should our focus be on what they're doing, but how to change it unequivocally; starting in our communities.

When I see you, I see me.

So, we've got to BLACK UP together!

The biggest part of our failure is not supporting each other on one accord. This divisive method of incendiary self-neglect will continue to perpetuate institutional racism, unless we *Wake Up*, and change the panoramic view to a cycloramic reality.

Boundaries

Don't let the boundary of what seems to be your physical condition dictate your faith. Your building should produce your challenge and the anticipation is in the seed that grows in you.

Every broken arm, skinned knee and broken elbow, all your blood, sweat and tears are in anticipation for your expectation.

The social injustices of constructional and instructional racism are not going anywhere. It's deeply seeded and inescapable in the DNA of college institutions.

Hence, every wish, dream and vision you have, God has already commenced the evolution for your provision. All you have to do is grow along with whatever you need toward that growth. Trust and never doubt; ask God again and again.

Never say to one's self, "I already did that." THAT'S DOUBT.

Just say, "God has not done it yet," and keep looking for it. Prayer is the key. Faith will unlock the door to all the roadblocks man has set up.

All God requires of you is for you to---believe it!

Quotes by Dr. Emanuel Officer

Words for Life

- Alternative facts will always embrace contradiction.

- Truth exposes plausible deniability.

- Chaos and distraction are just unpredictable plans.

- Ignorance is the most horrific mindset in the social construct of humanity.

- The inescapable, intrinsic things about us, will never leave us---not even at death.

- Negative words give you negative thoughts, negative thoughts give you negative ideas, negative ideas lead you to make negative choices. Negative choices put you in negative situations, negative situations will bring a negative outcome. Just replace positives wherever negatives are, and you will reach your greatest expectations.

- The most catastrophic, cataclysmic wrecking-ball in the construct of humanity is FEAR. It opens the door for paranoia, doubt, worry, unbelief, and insincerity. It will have you addicted to failure.

Therefore, remember this ... **"S.L.L."** ... Stop, Look, Listen ... before you commit yourself to the inheritance of any other person, place, or thing.

- At the crossroads of your life, everything is about your next step. Pay attention to the signs: Roadblock ... Bridge is out ... Dead End ... Do Not Enter ... and find your quickest route to success. Make sure your bearings are straight. One wrong turn can reroute your destination.

- When purpose and destiny line up, it will be harmonious. When your purpose does not meet destiny, you will be disconnected from the opportunity. Your potential must meet the protocol, and your opportunity must meet destiny. Then, the sky is the limit.

- Life is but a few fleeting moments. Therefore, what you do with the next few minutes makes all the difference in your life.

- Your persistence and determination create a powerful outcome.

- Focus your energy on the answers, not excuses. Eliminate what you don't need and be meticulous with everything that works for you.

- Anxiety is the contradiction of your humility. Don't take any short cuts to get around your greatness. A word for life.

- It's not the answer to the question; it's the question to your answer. Understanding what you're asking is more important than an answer which can't be questioned.

- To become who you are, you've got to go through the test. It's in the middle of your test that obstacles show. Maintain your focus; you will never get over any obstacles you don't confront. Obstacles will always come to roadblock your vision, but their truth in existing is to help you evolve and grow.

Words for life.

Chapter 8

Are You A Vessel of Strength?

There is no *try out* to be a member of *Vessels of Strength*. To be a *Vessel of Strength* you have to be an African American man, 18 years of age or older, and with a desire to enhance your life and support other, like-minded African American men.

You also have to be willing to teach, encourage and uplift your *Vessels of Strength* brothers. On the next page is a sample application to fill out and sign up, to become a Vessel of Strength. You may scan and e-mail us your application, or request an electronic copy.

vesselsofstrength@gmail.com

Thank you. God bless!

APPLICATION – GENERAL INFORMATION

Name: ________________________________

Phone Number: ________________________

Email Address: ________________________

Name of School(s) graduated from, attending or planning to attend: ________________________

____

If graduated, what year(s) and list of degree(s):

____

____

What is your major and minor (if applicable)?

____

____

Personal & Professional Goals to Accomplish as a *Vessel of Strength* Member: What do you desire to gain from *Vessels of Strength*?

____

____

What age group do you prefer your mentor to be? ________________. Why did you choose this age group?

____

____

____.

I, (*print name here*)________________________, agree that the information on this application has been completed to the best of my abilities.

________________________   ________________

Applicant's Signature   Date

About the Authors

Amber N. Hearn, DMFT

Dr. Hearn is a native of Los Angeles, California. Dr. Hearn's biological mother and father divorced when she was a child. Between the ages of 2 and 11, her mother was a single parent. During those years, Dr. Hearn and her mother experienced homelessness, while her mother battled systemic lupus erythematous. When Dr. Hearn was 11, her mother remarried and appreciated her stepfather for being, not only supportive to her mother, but also to her. She was a very ambitious student in elementary and high school and was involved in multiple leadership groups, such as the *Junior Daughters and Knights of St. Peter Claver*, and *Top Teens of America*. While in school, Dr. Hearn found herself experiencing challenges with completing assignments compared to her class- mates, but never knew why.

Despite these challenges, she maintained a 3.0 grade point average in high school. Dr. Hearn always wanted to help individuals and families by impacting their lives through psychology and Marriage and Family Therapy, whereupon she was introduced to Xavier University, Dillard University, and most honorable, the University of Arkansas at Pine Bluff (UAPB). It was always her dream to attend a Catholic, Historically Black College and University (HBCU), and Xavier University, in New Orleans, Louisiana, was her choice. In 2005, Dr. Hearn attended Xavier and felt as though she was in heaven, until the school announced an oncoming, catastrophic hurricane. It was Hurricane Katrina of 2005.

During the first week of school, her campus was evacuated out of New Orleans, whereupon she believed her dreams were crushed; until her mother reminded her of UAPB. Three weeks after the disastrous Hurricane Katrina hit New Orleans and flooded Xavier University, Dr. Hearn transferred to UAPB. She received financial, mentorship, and spiritual support, not only from UAPB, but also from Agricultural, Mechanical and Normal School (AM&N) AM&N/UAPB, Southern California Chapter Alumni Chapter in Los Angeles, California.

In the Spring of 2009, Dr. Hearn received her Bachelor of Science Degree in Psychology at the University of Arkansas at Pine Bluff, then. graduated from Drexel University in Philadelphia, Pennsylvania, in June 2011, with her Master of Family Therapy.

In the fall of 2012, Dr. Hearn was led by God to attend Loma Linda University, in California, for her Doctorate. During her doctoral journey, like a gift from above, Dr. Hearn had the opportunity to receive training in the fields of Program Development, Program Evaluation, Administration, Marketing, Marriage and Family Therapy, and grant writing, just to name a few. Along with this blessing, Dr. Hearn decided to explore her continued, personal challenges with completing assignments throughout her entire school experience.

During her self-exploratory years, Dr. Hearn was diagnosed with a reading disorder and was supported by a team of neuropsychologists who helped her through this process. Despite these challenges, with the guidance from the Lord, and those He sent to support her, Dr. Hearn received her Doctor of Marital and Family Therapy (DMFT) in 2016, with a concentration in Professional Consultation and Systems Relations, at Loma Linda University.

She gives all the glory to God! Not only is Dr. Hearn the founder of *Vessels of Strength*, she is also passionate about families who experience homelessness. Dr. Hearn was the lead author of two articles in the *Social History of the American Family Encyclopedia*, published by Sage Publication 2014; entitled: *Housing Crisis* and *Work and Family*. Dr. Hearn completed her doctorate by publishing her final DMFT project titled, *Breaking the Cycle of Homelessness: A Grounded Theory Needs Assessment*. **Note:** To read Dr. Hearn's published works, please e-mail: vesselsofstrength@gmail.com

Ernest Griffin, B.A.

Mr. Griffin is a native of Gardena, California. Raised by a single mother, his father had a part in his life. He graduated in 2012, and completed his Bachelor of Arts Degree in Communication, with a minor in Marketing. As he continues to work in the field of marketing, he plans to return to school to study Business Administration.

Phorode Brown, B.S.

Mr. Brown is a native of Bennettsville, South Carolina, and was raised by his family. In 2011, he graduated from Benedict College, a Historically Black College and University (HBCU), and received his Bachelor of Science Degree in Child and Family Development. At certain points in his college career at Benedict, he was acknowledged for his matriculation, not only academically, but also for service. Mr. Brown participated in various school programs, clubs, events and committees. Whether in the classroom, school events or public affairs, Phorode and other students received recognition for their hard work and progress. As he continues to work in the field of Child and Family Studies, he plans to return to college for his graduate degree in Psychology.

Emanuel Officer, Ph.D

Dr. Emanuel Officer is a native of Indianapolis, Indiana; the Midwest. "There were nine of us. I was the second from the youngest." His father was a truck driver for IU Medical Center and his mother cooked for Butler University. They didn't have much money, but his mother and father always made sure he and his sibling had clothes, shelter and food and a good education.

When Emanuel was in the sixth grade, his family moved to the suburbs from the city, whereupon he was placed into special education classes, to allot him the time to play catch-up until his senior year. Miraculously, young Emanuel graduated high school, and college was the last thing on his mind. However, in 1990, Emanuel picked up a book on Systematic Theology. Four years later, he enrolled in the Muskegon Bible Institute (MBI) in 2007. There, Emanuel received his Associate's Degree and felt compelled to continue his education, as he seemed to have entered a personal era of great enlightenment. He soon received his Bachelor's Degree in 2009. Still working toward his personal best, Emanuel then pursued a Masters' Degree.

In 2012, Emanuel earned a Doctorate of Divinity, followed by his Doctorate of Systematic Theology, and a Ph.D. in Philosophy, in 2015. Today, he is known as Dr. Officer, or Emanuel Officer, Ph.D. He counts Dr. Willie J Duncan as his greatest mentor.

Dr. Officer has written three published books: *A Word for Life: The Turning Point,* and *Finding Your Purpose;* and, at this writing, he's working on another two.

He is an existentialist and, like Immanuel Kant, Dr. Officer's hypothesis of incorporeal perceptual probability has opened an exhaustive range of knowledge without end. But he takes no credit, and deems his achievements as gifts, after being placed in special education. He appears regularly on the Power of Praise Network (PPN) streaming live on the *Church Spring Channel.*

Dr. Officer works from the Greek, Latin and Hebrew, the seven liberal arts and the geosciences during his teachings. He also accomplished little-known innovations in the music industry as a writer.

Dr. Officer believes his potential has met his protocol, to which, only the sky is the limit. His opportunity met its destiny. Today, Dr. Emanuel Wells Officer renders rich impartations to his readers and viewers.

Join Dr. Officer's Facebook page entitled, *Reconnecting to Black Consciousness.*

Note: To read Dr. Officer's published work, please e-mail:

vesselsofstrength@gmail.com

Bibliography

- M.B.I University. A WORD FOR LIFE. Facebook. URL: https://www.facebook.com/MbiUniversity/posts/1586420684767653; accessed July 21, 2019

- Harper, S. R. Black male student success in higher education: A report from the national Black male college achievement study. Philadelphia: University of Pennsylvania, Center for the Study of Race and Equity in Education, 2012.

- Suggs, E. HIGHER EDUCATION: Males a distinct minority at HBCUs: Historically Black College Campuses seek to boost numbers of Black men. The Atlanta Journal-Constitution, 2012.

- Vladimir Lenin Quotes. BrainyQuote.com, BrainyMedia Inc, 2019. URL: https://www.brainyquote.com/quotes/vladimir_lenin_132031; accessed July 21, 2019.

- Williamson, M. A. Return to love: Reflections on the principles of a course in miracles. Chapter 7: Work. (P.125). URL: https://digitalescobar.com/wp-content/uploads/2019/01/A-Return-to-Love-by; MarianneWilliamson_digitalescobar.com_.pdf; Accessed October 2, 2019.

- "Tulsa's Black Wall Street Flourished as a Self-Contained Hub in early 1900s. Updated September 16, 2019. Original September 4, 2019. URL: https://www.history.com/news/black-wall-street-tulsa-race-massacre

- Johnson, Robert and Cureton, Adam, "Kant's Moral Philosophy" The Stanford Encyclopedia of Philosophy (Spring 2019 Edition), Edward N. Zalta (ed.); URL: https://plato.stanford.edu/archives/spr2019/entries/kant-moral/

Acknowledgements

We thank God for giving us the strength, determination and diligence to complete this book. To our families and friends, we thank you for your encouragement. We'd also like to thank, the *Vessels of Strength Media* page supporters. And, special thanks to author, Brianna Whitaker, for volunteering her time to support our editing process; plus, Gail Barnes, owner of GK Printing, for designing the book cover; and Anne S. Hall for copy edits.

We look forward to connecting with you!

Visit us here:

Website:
www.vesselsofstrength.com

Email:
vesselsofstrength@gmail.com

Facebook:
https://www.facebook.com/AfricanAmericanMenVes
selsofStrength/

To order additional books, go to:

Amazon books Vessels of Strength